GW00375142

> **"** *...the desire to see with my own eyes, the world they call "Inland", to learn about Indian habits and customs, their needs, their belief, their religion and their language [...] won me over to make my way into their camps and to taste, before you, an ostrich-egg omelette at Nagüel Mapo.* **"**

Lucio V. Mansilla,
A Trip to the Ranquel Indians, 1870

Aguada Civilization

Other titles published by Maizal

Argentrip
Argentina's on-line travel guide
www.argentrip.com

© Christian le Comte, 2003
Book and Cover Design: Christian le Comte y Sophie le Comte
Photography: Christian le Comte y Sophie le Comte
Photography p. 22 de Jorge Schulte

Hecho el depósito que previene la ley 11.723
ISBN 987-9479-11-4
Published by Maizal
Muñiz 438, B1640FDB, Martínez
Buenos Aires, Argentina.
E-mail: info@maizal.com
www.maizal.com
Printed in September 2003 by Morgan Internacional.

Christian le Comte

Argentine Indians

MAIZAL
EDICIONES

Argentine Indians

The Indians, who originally inhabited what today is the Argentine Republic, belonged to different ethnic groups and the state of their evolution and culture varied according to the areas they lived in.

At the time of the discovery of America, when the Renaissance flourished in Europe, in Argentina many Indians still lived in the neolithic age.

The aborigines who inhabited the distant south belonged to nomadic tribes, they did not practice agriculture, had a very primitive social organization, did not know the art of pottery and were scantily clad in spite of the rigorous climate of Patagonia.

The settled tribes in the north, especially those that had been in contact with the Inca Empire, had learnt to cultivate the soil. They were skilful potters and had already begun to use metal as an ornament in their pottery although they did not know the existence of the potter's wheel. They had developed the arts of spinning and weaving. Their woollen clothes were woven in many colours. Their settled existence fostered the growth of institutions; the construction of sophisticated irrigation systems and cultivation platforms were no mean engineering feats. The plough was unknown in America, but these Indians were able to till the soil and keep flocks.

South American Indians used bow and arrows, some of them also used *boleadoras*, a weapon consisting of two large balls of wood or stone fastened to a third ball by means of strips of hide.

Most of them adopted the horse, which had been introduced by the conquerors, and became great horsemen. They then started using spears, which were dragged along the field leaving a raked track. The routes of the Pampas were built along these traces.

"Abipona", Martin Dobrizhoffer, 1783

The Indians used boleadoras to hunt. This weapon was later on adopted by the gauchos who used it with admirable dexterity.

Ornithomorphic pattern from a Sunchituyoc vase, Santiago del Estero, fifteenth century.

"Patagonian Cacique (chief) in battledress", E. Goupil, 1838

First Inhabitants

Sketch of the origin and distribution of the twelve species of men on earth by Ernst Haeckel, 1884, (detail)

The first inhabitants of America arrived more than 30.000 years ago.

During the Ice Ages, the level of the oceans fell and the Strait of Bering, which is only 45 m deep, dried off, joining America to Asia.

Crossing the Strait, waves of Asian groups began to invade America. From that moment on, every new wave of immigrants pushed the earlier ones southwards, driving them through North America towards South America.

The most imporant waves probably crossed between 25.000 and 11.000 BC.

Those who arrived in South America travelled about 8.000 kilometres in 7.000 years.

At the beginning, hunting was their main food source. Later on they fed on roots and fruits that grew wild in the forests. The oldest traces of these prehistoric cultures found in Tierra del Fuego are about 10.000 years old.

Scraper from Patagonia

The Route of the Atlantic

6.000-year-old scraper, used to clean leather.

There is a striking similarity between some tools used by some cultures in Southwest Europe and those used by the Indians in North America. This has made historians think about the possibility of a migration across the North Atlantic.

The Vikings probably arrived in America in the twelfth and thirteenth centuries, but they did not influence American culture in any way.

Transpacific Connections

A series of factors lead to suppose that America could have been invaded from the west by people who used the routes across the Pacific Ocean.

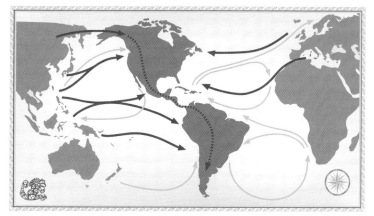

Certain racial and cultural similarities exist among the inhabitants of Australia and Southeast Asia, and the inhabitants of South America.

Although it seems impossible, given the immense distances, these similarities induce to contemplate the possibility.

The ocean current of Kuro–Shivo, which originates in the Philippines and Japan, reaches California; the currents from Polynesia and New Zealand that move towards Chile and Peru in South America and the Ecuadorian counter current are among the natural factors that were probably taken advantage of by Asian navigators.

The western winds were also a help to some tribes who had developed an ability to sail.

→ *Ocean Currents and Winds*
➞ *Migrations*

The Cave of the Hands

*25 mm long
Palaeolithic
arrowhead*

The Cave of the Hands is located in a deep canyon that the river Pinturas eroded in the stone, 71 km south of the city of Perito Moreno in the Province of Santa Cruz.

The name originates in the drawings of more than thousand hands that, like negative impressions, cover the rock.

They are painted in white, black, ochre, violet, yellow and red and the pigments used are a mixture of powder of stones found in the region and guanaco fat. These hands, probably depicted around 550 BC, have the striking characteristic of being white.

Most of these impressions are in a 24 m long cave and the people who painted them were hunters and gatherers.

*The length of this type
of arrowheads ranges
between 20 and 50 mm*

Apart from the hands, there are drawings representing animals and geometric designs. The oldest painting, which depicts guanacos facing a hunter, is 9.000 years old. Around the year 1000 BC a tribe painted the geometric figures and the positive impressions of the hands.

Cerro Colorado (Red Hill)

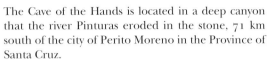

*Arrowhead found in
Patagonia (60 mm)*

In 1902, the poet Leopoldo Lugones discovered paintings on the hills in the Sierra de Ambargasta in the Province of Córdoba. Two different tribes, the Sanavirones and the Comechingones, covered the place with more than 35.000 drawings.

Scenes of battles and hunting, animals, plants and even Spanish conquerors on horseback have been drawn on the red rock.

Pre–Columbian Art

The agrarian cultures, that manufactured pottery in the northwest of Argentina, started their development at the beginning of the Christian era. The objects found are mainly tools for domestic use or those related to religious purposes. What today is considered a work of art can scarcely have been produced for the sake of creating beautiful objects. The production of pottery can be divided into three periods:

Alamito Condorhuasi Civilization mortar

I. EARLY PERIOD (up to AD 650).
The objects are mainly grey and black. The pieces of this period are grouped according to the archaeological sites in which they were found.

Candelaria: This pottery is mainly grey and its most striking characteristic is the representation of the human body with bulging forms (southern Salta and northern Tucumán).

Condorhuasi: The objects found in this area have an incise decoration. Besides pottery, these tribes had attained technical skill in metalworking.
The colours used are red, white and black with incise geometric ornaments. The designs include fantastic animals that combine anatomical features of different species. There are statues of seated or crawling human beings. Paintings of men clad in tunics with strange headdresses represent the sun (western Catamarca).

Ciénaga: These ceramic vases are mainly black, decorated with triangles and zigzag fringes. In a later period they also include drawings of felines, batrachians and lamas (Calchaquí Valleys).

Vaquería: The ceramic is red and black on a beige background. The representation of the jaguar is related to the sun, considered a god by these tribes (Jujuy and Salta).

II. MIDDLE PERIOD (from AD 650 to AD 900)

The pieces found in the Provinces of Catamarca and La Rioja belong to a period of artistic relevance.

Aguada or Draconiana: *This ceramic has anthropomorphic decoration (with characteristic oblique position of eyes and monstrous face).*

The vases have incise and painted animal ornaments in various colours. They are of medium size, thin walls and excellent finish.

Vase with anthropomorphic decoration, Aguada Ambato

III. LATE PERIOD (from AD 850 to AD 1480).

This pottery has Inca influence with felines and snakes painted with a zigzag pattern. The arrival of the conquerors put an end to this culture.

Angualasto: *The ceramic vases found in this region are red with black ornaments of wavy fringes, triangles and anthropomorphic decorations in relief.*

Belén: *This pottery has drawings and engravings of double-headed snakes. The polished ware is of reddish colour engraved with black pictures (Catamarca and north of La Rioja).*

Condorhuasi Civilization

Santa María: *The decoration is characterized by the repetition of the same picture; in the centre of the vases there are animals such as the ñandú (South American ostrich), the toad or the snake (Catamarca and north of La Rioja).*

San José: *The vases and urns found in this site have colourful decorations.*

p. 10 anthropomorphic figure, Vaquerías Civilization

Besides the pottery of the Provinces of the northwest, other manifestations of less importance have been found in northern Argentina: the statuettes found in the Sierra de Córdoba, the bird like pieces of the River Paraná Medio and the urns with geometric drawings of the Guaraní civilization called Arroyo Malo (after ad 1200).

Hunters of the South

"Yámana Indian"
Conrad Martens,
1833

*In 1584, around 300
people disembarked in
the desolate coast of the
of the Magellan Strait
to found a town. Two
and a half years later,
Cavendish, the English
pirate, found only 18
survivors.
The place was called
Puerto Hambre (Port
Hunger).*

The Selk'nam and the Haush who inhabited the southeastern end of the Isla Grande de Tierra del Fuego.

These nomadic tribes adapted to one of the most rigorous climates on earth, with strong winds and winters of -20°C. To protect themselves, they wore animal skins. They hunted guanacos, foxes, rodents and birds and gathered fruits and roots. A stranded whale was sometimes the occasion for a banquet on the beach, which could last for weeks. They did not form permanent establishments but groups of 50 to 100 people built their tents together. The tents were light and so easy to put up, that sometimes it was easier to move the tents to the place where the prey had been found than to move the prey to the tent. To show their mood they painted their faces with earth and fat. They lived in peace with their neighbours the Yámanas and the Alacaluf.

These tribes that occupied the whole island of Tierra del Fuego, no longer exist.

The Hain

*Harpoon used by
Canoeists of the
Magellan Strait*

The *hain* was an initiation rite that could last for months. Men got together with the initiate to teach him how to scare women. He then participated in the "secret". The farce of this representation could not be disclosed so that men could maintain supremacy over women. Men did not want to loose this supremacy because they knew that it had been the other way round in the past.

Canoeists of the End of the World

There were two canoeist tribes: the Yámanas or Yahganes who inhabited the coast of the Beagle Channel and the islands of the Magellanic Archipelago, and the Alakaluf, who inhabited the southern tip of Chile.

"Head of Patagón"
Moritz Rugendas,
(1802-1858)

The Yámanas spent most of their time in their canoes made of beech bark kept together with vegetable fibres, so most of them had weak legs and highly developed arms. While the men hunted from the canoe, women had to row and the children took care of the fire that had to be kept burning inside the canoe. With their bone-tipped harpoons they hunted marine mammals. They also gathered shellfish: clams, mussels, crabs and sea hedgehogs and they hunted otters and marine birds, especially cormorants.

They slept in tents made of branches and skins, which looked towards the sea.

Although these nomadic tribes led very primitive lives, their striking characteristic was their language, which had more than 35.000 words.

Every time a European ship got near the coast, the Selk'nam or Onas lit huge fires as an emergency signal. It is due to these fires that the travellers called the place Tierra del Fuego, (Earth of Fire).

"Yámanas in the Beagle Channel",
Conrad Martens,
1834

Giants of the South

"French Sailor and Patagonian Family" (detail), Dom Pernetty, 1765

Patagonia extends from the River Colorado to Cape Horn and from the Andes to the Atlantic Ocean and it covers an area of approximately 1.000.000 km².

The name of Patagonia originated in the legend invented by some travellers who described the land as being inhabited by gigantic men who had extraordinary big feet. Pata means foot, hence the curious name.

Antonio Pigafetta, the chronicler of Magellan's expedition (1519–1522) is said to be responsible for the legend. *"One day, unexpectedly, a man of gigantic figure appeared before us. He was standing on the sand, almost naked, and he sang and danced at the same time…this man was so big that our head hardly reached his waist…"*

The Jesuit Thomas Falkner, sent in 1740 to Patagonia, lived with them. It was Falkner who threw light on the subject: although the Patagonian Indians were high, they were by no means giants.

These tribes can be divided into two groups, those of the south, called Chonik and those of the north called Puelche-Guénaken. The Chonik were nomadic tribes that hunted guanacos and ostriches. They used bows, arrows, boleadoras and stones and camouflaged themselves with feathers and branches.

Their huts made of branches and large skins protected them from the strong, biting wind.

Indians of North Patagonia

The Puelche–Guénaken lived in the region of the rivers Colorado (Red River) and Negro (Black River) and sometimes they even got as far as the Sierra de Tandil and the Sierra de la Ventana. For this reason they were also called *Serranos* (Mountain People).

According to Nuño da Sylva, Francis Drake anchored close to the Patagonian shore in 1578, some Indians with painted faces approached him. One of them separated from the group and unexpectedly stole Drake's hat.

Drake in Puerto Deseado, engraving by Johann de Bry, 1594

As their neighbours the Chonik, they led a nomadic life, hunting guanacos and ñandus. They also gathered roots and seeds and they knew how to prepare alcoholic drinks. Alcide D'Orbigny, a French traveller, wrote in his chronicle: "these Indians had a broad and serious face".

Their dress was the *quillango*, a coloured blanket of fox or guanaco skin and a loincloth. They painted their faces and they used a *vincha* (head band).

Their huts were built of timber covered with skins with the hair on the outside. They lived in groups of about one hundred families led by a *cacique* (chief).

After the Conquest, the Puelches were invaded by the Mapuche Indians from whom they learnt how to break in a horse and the use of the spear to attack settlements along the frontier.

Anonymous engraving representing a Patagonian Indian eating arrows, 1603

The Indians of the Pampas

Araucanian pectoral ornament (trapelacuche)

Earrings used both by men and women

The Pampas were originally inhabited by Querandí Indians, also called Pampas. They were mainly deer hunters, who used to run after their prey to tire it out. When the deer slackened their pace, the Indians leapt and caught them by their feet.

Their weapons were the bow, the arrow and the boleadoras. They were the first Indians to meet the conquerors when Pedro de Mendoza arrived to found the city of Buenos Aires in 1536.

The Pampas were also inhabited by the Mapuches (mapu: earth and che: people) as they called themselves. The Spaniards called them Araucanos because they came from the valley of Arauca in Chile. They invaded the Pampas to steal horses and moved by the interest to come into contact with the Spaniards. Eventually they displaced the Querandíes.

The Mapuches dressed themselves in a loincloth and a poncho, woven by their women, and they used a vincha on their head; women covered themselves with guanaco blankets. Their huts were simple

Araucanian pectoral ornament

pieces of horse leather stretched on branches called toldos; a group of these huts was a toldería, a camp. They believed in a supreme being and in an evil spirit called Gualichu.

Towards the end of the nineteenth century, most of the Pampas were in their hands. In order to defend their land, they constantly harassed military forts and frontier settlements.

After several attempts to stop these attacks, General Julio A. Roca organized the most important expedition against the Indians in 1879: "the Campaign to the Desert". After this military operation, the territory was extended, the frontier was moved many miles into the Pampas and cattle breeding became the most important activity.

Today the Mapuches are approximately 200.000 and they live mainly in the Provinces of Río Negro, Neuquén and Chubut where they keep their traditions, which have been incorporated to the educational system.

Since March 2001 the Mapuche language is taught at schools in their communities in Neuquén.

Araucanian silver pectoral ornament (shikil)

Head ornament (trarilonko)

Araucanian earring (upul)

Pampas, Emeric Essex Vidal, 1817p. 16 "Buenos Aires", Utz Schmidl, Levinus Hulsius, 1602

The Horse and the Indian

Alarm in the Pampas
When the Indians, lay in wait in the Pampas, ready to attack, they were very careful not to bother the ñandu (ostrich). As soon as the ñandu detected Indian presence, it immediately began to run and alerted the other animals and the commotion spread all over the place. These animals' movements were visible in the plain and they were a clear sign that the Indians were near.

Of all Indian groups in Argentina, the Mapuches were the best horsemen. The horse, brought by the Spaniards, reproduced itself quickly and a big amount of horse herds roamed freely over the Pampas. The horse was then incorporated to the life of the Indians who took advantage of it: they ate its meat, they drank its blood; with its leather they covered their huts, manufactured lassos, reins and other pieces of their saddle and women sewed with their tendons. Lucio V. Mansilla in his famous book *A Trip to the Ranquel Indians* writes: *"The Indians have the habit of resting on the horse. They lie down on it as if it were a bed, putting their head on the neck of the animal, and extending the crossed legs on the haunches; they remain like this for a while, sometimes for hours. They do not get off the horse, not even when it is thirsty, they can take off the bit and put it back again sitting on the saddle. Their animals are not only exceptionally strong but very docile as well. Is the Indian asleep? The horse does not move. Is he drunk? It helps him keep the balance. He gets off and lowers the rein? It stays where it is. How long? The whole day.*
The Indians live on their horses, as fishermen in their boats: Their element are the Pampas, as the element of the fishermen is the sea."

"Travelling Indians",
Theodor Ohlsen, 1894

The Malón

The *malón* was the attack by surprise of Indians who sacked the frontier area.

Cunningham Graham in his book *The Río de la Plata* of 1870, describes it in the following way: *"... the Indians exploded, as if a ray would burst among the clouds in*

the fields inland, with the fury of a pampero [dry wind] that blows from the South [...] Their raids always followed the same roads, very well-known to the gauchos who called them malones; they often made incursions into the Province of Buenos Aires [...] an atmosphere of legend and terror floated around their settlements. When they invaded the big estancias [farms] of the South, except for their chief, they all rode on a piece of leather and more often that not on the bare horse, with their 20 feet long tacuara spear, [...] on their way deer and ostriches escaped like marine foam flying over huge waves. [...] Riding like demons in the darkness, exciting their horses with the fury of their attack and crossing small streams [...] slipping away in the scrubland with the noise of tramped reeds. The horsemen hit their mouths with their hands while giving never ending and terrifying cries..."

The Mapuches had a magic recipe for their horses to be excellent runners. They took the feather of an eagle (that had to be set free later on) and burnt it. The ashes, dissolved in water were given to the newborn foal.

"The return of the malón", Ángel Della Valle, 1892

The women taken by a malón were called "captives". These women never returned to town not even if they had the chance to escape. It was out of shame or because they had formed a new family in captivity.

"The Captive", M. Rugendas, 1845

Mesopotamia and Gran Chaco

"Mocobí Indian" and "Río Paraguay" (p. 21), F. Paucke SJ, (1719-1779)

"Abipones hunting" F. Assner, 1763

During their magic rites, the Matacos inhaled cebil, a narcotic substance, which they took from the Norco Cebil tree (Parapiptadenia sublime). The roasted seed, reduced to powder, could also be smoked.

Birdlike figure of the Paraná River

The Argentine Mesopotamia extends along the riverbanks of the Uruguay and the Paraná rivers.

The Indians of this area used to fish from canoes and they ate dried off and smoked fish. They hunted otters and deer and they gathered honey in the

forests. Shortly before the conquerors arrived, they had started toiling the soil. Some of the tribes had begun using ceramic vases with incise decoration and handles with animal shapes. Their huts were small shacks.

From south to north, the tribes in this area were: Timbúes, Carcaraes, Mberguaes, Chanaes, Mocoretaes. The Charrúa Indians came from the oriental riverbank of the Río de la Plata.

The Chaco, a region in north-eastern Argentina, was inhabited by the Guaycurú group formed by the Mocobíes, Abipones, Tobas, Pilegaes and to the west, the Matacos. They were nomadic tribes, hunters and gatherers, mainly of the fruit of the algarrobo (*Prosopis nigra*). The Guaycurú Indians were taller and more belligerent than their neighbours the Matacos.

Guaraní Indians

The Guaraní tribes came from the region of the Amazon River and they moved to Misiones, Chaco and Formosa where the Guaraní language is still spoken today.

"The Mission of San Miguel", A. Demersai, 1846

p. 22: Ruins of San Ignacio, Misiones by Jorge Schulte

These tribes lived in villages made up of large communal houses and several families inhabited each house. They usually remained for five or six years in the same place where they practiced agriculture by raking the land because the plough was unknown to American Indians. They sowed corn, sweet potatoes, manioc, pumpkins and vegetables. Men devoted themselves to hunting, using the bow and arrow and to fishing from big canoes.

Women spun cotton, which was woven in simple vertical looms and manufatured big ceramic vases to store chicha, an alcoholic drink prepared from the fruit of the algarrobo.

They believed in a God called Tupá, the Creator, who, according to the legend, had given them the *mate* tree (*Ilex paraguayensis*) that grows in the Guaraní forest. The Guaraní Indians prepared a tea using the dry leaves of *mate*.

The Jesuits arrived in America at the beginning of the sixteenth century to teach the native Indians the Christian doctrine. They began their work at the Guaraní missions in 1578. The egalitarian principles of the Jesuits collided with the colonialist ideas of the Spanish Crown and they were expelled from Argentina in 1767.

The historian Lucía Gálvez compares the Creation Hymn of the Guaraní Indians to the first part of Saint John's Gospel: "Of the wisdom contained in his sky-being, by virtue of his knowledge that opens up like a flower, our Father opened the fundamental word and made the world like himself, divine sky thing…"

Central Area

*Bird-like design
Sunchituyoc,
Santiago del Estero*

The Comechingones (name that imitates their war cry) of Córdoba built their houses under the earth's surface. They were brown, high and were the only tribe in the whole country who had a beard. This characteristic differentiates them from all other tribes and it is thought that their origin is different. The Incas did not influence them, yet they knew how to cultivate corn, beans and pumpkins. They spun and wove lama wool and modelled ceramic vases in baskets so that they kept their form and decoration.

The Lules and Vilelas of Tucumán were nomadic tribes. They were also called Juríes, (quichua name for ostrich), because they were very tall and thin.

*Table mat with
decorations of
coloured cornhusk*

The Tonocotés of Santiago del Estero devoted themselves to agriculture. The round huts covered with straw are a characteristic of this tribe. They celebrated long religious festivities drinking an alcoholic beverage prepared from *algarrobo* and corn.

The Sanavirones of the south of Santiago lived in big houses surrounded by huge cacti called *cardones*. Each hut was inhabited by several families.

Andean Tribes

*Menhirs of Tafí del
Valle, Tucumán*

*p. 25: "Inhabitants of
the Río de la Plata or
Tucumán", Woodes
Rogers, 1716*

The belligerent Pehuenches who lived in the region of the Nahuel Huapí were hunters. They gathered the fruit of the *pehuén* (*Araucaria araucana*) with which they made their bread. The peaceful, intelligent and agile Huarpes from Cuyo and the Olongastas from La Rioja led a settled life. They had learnt from the Incas how to build a stronghold called *pucará*, to cultivate corn and *quinua*, and to use watering systems built on the slopes of the mountains.

Inca Influence

"Indian Spinning",
Guamán Poma de
Ayala, 1587

Anthropomorphic
figure, Santa María

Anthropomorphic
figure, Santa María

The Cochinocas, divided into three groups called Omahuacas, Tilcaras and Purmamarcas, lived in the northern area of the northwest along the eastern border of the Puna (the high desert plateau in northern Argentina) and occupied the Quebrada of Humahuaca (Ravine of Humahuaca), a valley that links the high plateau in the north and the plains of the south. They were hard-working tribes who built irrigation systems and supporting walls for their cultivation platforms. They knew how to till the soil with shovels and to keep the crops in silos. The houses were made of stone and the roof was made of a mixture of mud and pebbles. They had big flocks of lamas, which they used as a means of transport.

They were dressed in the typical tunic called *unku* used by all Andean tribes. This vicuña or lama wool dress was long and reached their ankles. They also used ponchos and blankets to protect themselves from the cold. They fastened their ponchos with long woollen belts. Their footwear, called *ojota*, was made of raw lama leather. They used bracelets, rings, tupos and colourful beads made of lapis lazuli and malachite stones.

The inhabitants of the *Quebrada* were skilful potters. The geometric and animal patterns are mainly black, red or white.

The Omahuacas were brave warriors and they were the last tribe to subdue to the system of the Spanish conquerors. They were shrewd strategists and they carefully prepared for war. Their *pucarás* served them as a refuge in the mountain in case of attack.

The Incan cult of the sun and the moon was introduced in the middle of the fifteenth century as the Inca Empire started to expand.

The Inhabitants of the Puna

The Apatamas were a peaceful, sedentary tribe. As most of the Andean inhabitants, they cultivated the

earth and kept their crops in caves. They dressed in the typical Andean tunic and their ponchos had geometric drawings. Today, the inhabitants of the Puna still use the distinctive colourful wool caps of the Apatamas.

Since they had access to immense salt mines, they supplied the neighbouring tribes with salt.

Pucará of Tilcara
The pucará was a stronghold in the mountain where the Indians took refuge in case of attack.

The Diaguitas and Calchaquíes had attained a variety of outstanding skills. They were able to grind the seeds of the algarrobo to prepare flour, which was kept in underground silos. They also were excellent ceramists and developed skills in metalworking, flattening pieces of copper, brass, silver and gold with big stones.

Diaguitas and Calchaquíes

These belligerent Indians had the most highly developed culture in Argentina. They were divided into several groups such as Hualfines, Pulares, Tolombones, Quilmes, Yocaviles and they inhabited the Andean valleys of the northwest, subdued by the Inca Empire. They cultivated corn, beans, pumpkins and quinua. They built watering systems and platforms on the hillsides of the mountains. The canals built by the Cacanes, a collective name for these tribes, are still used today.

Ornithtomorphic bowl, Inca period

The Wichis

Caraguatá, (Bromelia hieronymi), plant of the western forest of Formosa

"Clay Pottery"
Florian Paucke S J,
(1719-1779)

Yica, handbag knitted with caraguatá fibre

Duck carved in palo santo wood (Bulnesia sarmientoi) with bone inlaid

A community of about 80.000 Wichis, (*wichi* means people in their language) still live in the area of the Great Chaco. They belong to one of the eldest tribes in the region. Originally they were gatherers of *algarrobo*,

prickly pear, pumpkins and honey. They hunted with bows and arrows and fished with harpoons.

Today the Wichis devote themselves to the manufacture of wooden objects and they specialize in spinning the thread cut from the leaves of the chaguar.

The chaguar or caraguatá (a bromelia that grows in the forests of Chaco, in the northeast) is used by the Wichis as food, medicine, magic object and to produce the fibre used for their fabrics.

To produce this fibre, the leaves are gathered in the forest, cut and dried off in the sun. Then they are twisted and coloured with algarrobo (*Prosopis nigra*) bark, quebracho (*Schinopsis quebracho colorado*) or palo santo (*Bulnesia sarmientoi*). With this fibre women knit *yicas* (handbags), strings and hammocks.

The Poncho

The Pampas and the Indians of northern Argentina covered themselves with the poncho and each tribe incorporated their symbols to the woven material. In the north, vicuña wool was used and the ponchos had different shades of beige that corresponded to the wool of the different parts of the animal. The rhombus pattern used in the ponchos from the north represent the sun and originated in Bolivia and Peru.

The ponchos from Catamarca are embroidered with flowers and their colourful fringes have Spanish influence. The ponchos from Chaco have geometric patterns: zigzags, triangles and rhombuses.

The Mapuches incorporated zigzags that resemble steps which are connected to the form in which they see the universe: divided into four regions. In the centre of the patterns there are crosses which are related to their ideas of the ascent to heaven.

The ponchos of Jesuitical influence are called "of thousand lines" and they are characteristic of the region between the Paraná and Uruguay rivers.

Poncho woven in the Province of Jujuy

Poncho woven in San Carlos, (Salta)

The pattern with the condor was used in textiles because it was believed that if one saw a condor while sowing, the harvest would be excellent.

*"Patagonian Indians"
Emille Lasalle, 1829*

The Conquest

After the arrival of the conquerors, life changed drastically. As the Indians were free vassals of the King of Castile, they were forced to pay a tribute to the king.

To compensate the conquerors, who had spent a lot of money organizing the expeditions, it was determined that they would receive that tribute, and not the king. This tribute had to be paid either in money, goods or labour. The Indians were forced to pay in labour.

Conquerors by Théodore de Bry, 1602

Although the Laws of the Indies were based on a generous policy of the Crown, big injustices were committed because of the limitless wealth ambition of many conquerors.

After the conquest, the Indian elite was incorporated to society and they mixed with the Spaniards. Many Indians moved to the cities, others worked in the fields or in mines or they devoted themselves to their arts and crafts.

Today some 700 Indian communities are scattered throughout the whole country.

The Argentine Constitution maintains that the country "*acknowledges the pre-existent ethnic and cultural communities in Argentina; guarantees the respect for their identity and the right to a bilingual and intercultural education and recognizes the legal status of their communities, and the communal possession and property of the land that they have traditionally occupied*". (art. 75)

Oceanica Classis

Illustration of a book of travels to South America

Illustration of the travels of Walter Raleigh, 1599

Apatamas Matacos
Cochinocas Wichis
Pilagaes
Tobas
Mocovíes
Tonocotés Guaraníes
Abipones
Lules
Diaguitas Mocoretaes
Sanavirones Chanaes
Mbeguaes
Carcaraes Charrúas
Comechingones Timbúes

Huarpes Querandíes

Pampas
Ranqueles
Mapuches

Pehuenches
Puelches

Chónik

INDIAN
TRIBES

Alacaluf
Yámanas
Selk'nam
(Onas)

Index